PAUL REVERE'S RIDE

Paul Revere's Ride

HENRY WADSWORTH LONGFELLOW

illustrations by
PAUL GALDONE

Thomas Y. Crowell Company · New York

To Joanna and Paul Ferenc

PAUL REVERE'S RIDE

LISTEN, my children, and you shall hear
Of the midnight ride of Paul Revere,
On the eighteenth of April, in 'Seventy-five;
Hardly a man is now alive
Who remembers that famous day and year.

He said to his friend, "If the British march
By land or sea from town to-night,
Hang a lantern aloft in the belfry arch
Of the North Church tower as a signal light,—
One, if by land, and two, if by sea;

And I on the opposite shore will be,
Ready to ride and spread the alarm
Through every Middlesex village and farm,
For the country-folk to be up and to arm."

Then he said, "Good night!" and with muffled oar
Silently rowed to the Charlestown shore,
Just as the moon rose over the bay,
Where swinging wide at her moorings lay
The Somerset, British man-of-war;

A phantom ship, with each mast and spar
Across the moon like a prison bar,
And a huge black hulk, that was magnified
By its own reflection in the tide.

Meanwhile, his friend, through alley and street,
Wanders and watches with eager ears,
Till in the silence around him he hears
The muster of men at the barrack door,
The sound of arms, and the tramp of feet,
And the measured tread of the grenadiers,
Marching down to their boats on the shore.

Then he climbed to the tower of the church,
Up the wooden stairs, with stealthy tread,
To the belfry-chamber overhead,
And startled the pigeons from their perch
On the sombre rafters, that round him made
Masses and moving shapes of shade,—
Up the trembling ladder, steep and tall,
To the highest window in the wall,

Where he paused to listen and look down
A moment on the roofs of the town,
And the moonlight flowing over all.

Beneath, in the churchyard, lay the dead,
In their night-encampment on the hill,
Wrapped in silence so deep and still
That he could hear, like a sentinel's tread,
The watchful night-wind, as it went
Creeping along from tent to tent,
And seeming to whisper, "All is well!"
A moment only he feels the spell
Of the place and the hour, and the secret dread
Of the lonely belfry and the dead;

For suddenly all his thoughts are bent
On a shadowy something far away,
Where the river widens to meet the bay,—
A line of black that bends and floats
On the rising tide, like a bridge of boats.

Meanwhile, impatient to mount and ride,
Booted and spurred, with a heavy stride
On the opposite shore walked Paul Revere.
Now he patted his horse's side,
Now gazed at the landscape far and near,
Then, impetuous, stamped the earth,
And turned and tightened his saddle-girth;

But mostly he watched with eager search
The belfry-tower of the Old North Church,
As it rose above the graves on the hill,
Lonely and spectral and sombre and still.

And lo! as he looks, on the belfry's height
A glimmer, and then a gleam of light!

He springs to the saddle, the bridle he turns,
But lingers and gazes, till full on his sight
A second lamp in the belfry burns!

A hurry of hoofs in a village street,
A shape in the moonlight, a bulk in the dark,
And beneath, from the pebbles, in passing, a spark
Struck out by a steed flying fearless and fleet;
That was all! And yet, through the gloom and the light,
The fate of a nation was riding that night;
And the spark struck out by that steed, in his flight,
Kindled the land into flame with its heat.

He has left the village and mounted the steep,
And beneath him, tranquil and broad and deep,
Is the Mystic, meeting the ocean tides;
And under the alders, that skirt its edge,
Now soft on the sand, now loud on the ledge,
Is heard the tramp of his steed as he rides.

It was twelve by the village clock
When he crossed the bridge into Medford town.
He heard the crowing of the cock,
And the barking of the farmer's dog,
And felt the damp of the river fog,
That rises after the sun goes down.

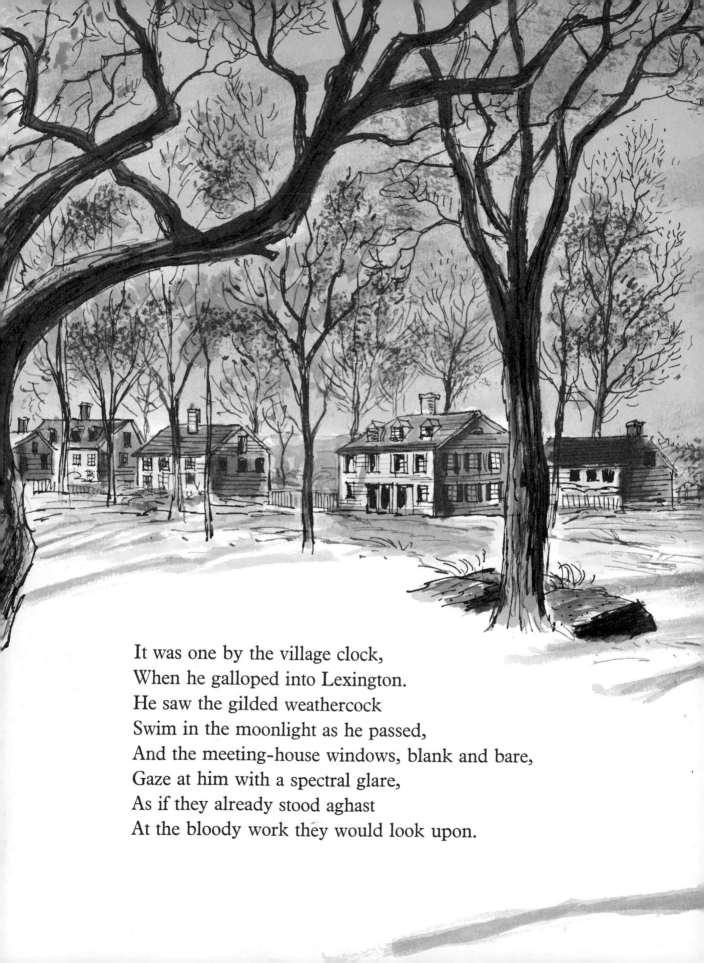

It was one by the village clock,
When he galloped into Lexington.
He saw the gilded weathercock
Swim in the moonlight as he passed,
And the meeting-house windows, blank and bare,
Gaze at him with a spectral glare,
As if they already stood aghast
At the bloody work they would look upon.

It was two by the village clock,
When he came to the bridge in Concord town.
He heard the bleating of the flock,
And the twitter of birds among the trees,
And felt the breath of the morning breeze
Blowing over the meadows brown.
And one was safe and asleep in his bed
Who at the bridge would be first to fall,
Who that day would be lying dead,
Pierced by a British musket-ball.

You know the rest. In the books you have read,
How the British Regulars fired and fled,—
How the farmers gave them ball for ball,
From behind each fence and farm-yard wall,
Chasing the red-coats down the lane,
Then crossing the fields to emerge again
Under the trees at the turn of the road,
And only pausing to fire and load.

So through the night rode Paul Revere;
And so through the night went his cry of alarm
To every Middlesex village and farm,—
A cry of defiance and not of fear,
A voice in the darkness, a knock at the door,
And a word that shall echo forevermore!
For, borne on the night-wind of the Past,
Through all our history, to the last,
In the hour of darkness and peril and need,
The people will waken and listen to hear
The hurrying hoof-beats of that steed,
And the midnight message of Paul Revere.

Longfellow House
Cambridge, Mass.

ABOUT THE AUTHOR

Although Henry Wadsworth Longfellow did not write specifically for young people, many of his lyric and narrative poems are profoundly appealing to them. *The Wreck of the Hesperus*, *Evangeline*, *The Courtship of Miles Standish*, *Hiawatha*, *A Psalm of Life* (to name a few) are considered standard introductions to poetry—and often to American history.

"Paul Revere's Ride" is one of a collection of twenty-one long narrative poems in *Tales of a Wayside Inn*, published in 1863. The book is similar in form to Chaucer's *Canterbury Tales* and Boccaccio's *Decameron*, for each tale is narrated by a member of a group gathered around a fireside in a New England tavern.

Longfellow was born in Portland, Maine, in 1807. In his time, he was renowned not only as a writer but as a professor of modern languages, first at Bowdoin College (from which he had been graduated) and later at Harvard. He continued to teach until 1854, when he resigned to devote himself to the literary life. In 1884, two years after Longfellow's death, his bust was placed in the Poets' Corner of Westminster Abbey. He was the first American to be commemorated there.

ABOUT THE ILLUSTRATOR

During the preparation of his illustrations for *Paul Revere's Ride*, Paul Galdone spent a good deal of time in the area of Massachusetts described in the poem. Through the kindness of the vicar at the famous Old North Church, he was allowed to climb the legendary steeple to view the terrain during the same season in which the ride took place. His research also took him to Paul Revere's home, to museums in Boston and Concord, and along the route of Revere's ride.

Paul Galdone is considered one of the outstanding illustrators of children's books today. He studied at the Art Students League in New York and with George Grosz. Much of his spare time is spent in sketching from life in public places and the countryside.

Mr. Galdone came to the United States as a boy from Budapest, Hungary. He now lives in Rockland County, New York, with his wife and two children.

14288